All I Know Is What's on TV

All I Know Is What's on TV

By
Bill Walraven

Illustrated by John C. Davis Jr.

Javelina Press
Corpus Christi, Texas

Javelina Press
P.O. Box 1479
Corpus Christi, TX 78403
(512)-992-8031

ISBN 0-9646325-0-0

To my mother, Valerie Garrison Walraven, who lived the rigors of frontier life in Indian Territory and who deserved better than life gave her.

Her hero was William Penn Adair Rogers, even though she never knew his full name. She knew his country and understood his roots and, like millions of others, considered him family.

—Bill Walraven

By Bill Walraven:

Humor:

Real Texans Don't Drink Scotch in Their Dr Pepper
Walraven's World or Star (Boarder) and Other Wars

History:

Corpus Christi: History of a Texas Seaport
El Rincón: A History of Corpus Christi Beach

With Marjorie K. Walraven:

The Magnificent Barbarians: Little-Told Tales of the Texas
Revolution

"I have often said, in answer to inquiries as to how I got away with kidding some of our public men, that it was because I like all of them personally, and that if there was no malice in your heart there could be none in your 'gags'"—*June 29, 1930*

"Those denouncing orators should remember every time they cuss a President, they lose friends. They may get applause from a partisan audience, but we still think its the highest office in the whole world.
  "So any denouncer—no matter which side he is on—loses more votes than he gains."—*June 9, 1935*

"When I die, my epitaph or whatever you call those signs on gravestones is going to read: 'I joked about every prominent man of my time, but I never met a man I dident like.' I am so proud of that I can hardly wait to die so it can be carved. And when you come to my grave you will find me sitting there, proudly reading it."—*June 16, 1930.*

—*Will Rogers*

Contents

'We can't start yet, man. The TV crews won't show up
for another fifteen minutes.'

Preface

Will Rogers used to say, "All I know is what I read in the papers."

He'd be in bad shape with tabloid journalism. If he were getting his information from today's press, he'd have a hard time learning about some major stories: rip-offs of the environment and the Social Security trust fund; scandals in housing, savings and loans, and banking; chicanery in dealings between business and government leaders; and other important subjects.

But he'd have full knowledge of Lorena and John Wayne Bobbitt, Clarence Thomas and Anita Hill, Paula Jones, Gennifer Flowers, President Clinton's underwear, and O.J. Simpson.

He'd think he was on another planet. Today he'd see fiction, opinion, and entertainment, all mixed up. He'd see rumors and accusations without proof or attribution. He'd read whole pages and find nothing of substance.

Will wouldn't be as smart as he was in his day, but he'd have a lot of material to joke about.

As a newspaper columnist who turned out five columns a week, I often thought of Will Rogers and what a huge talent he was, writing columns even when he was in the middle of filming a movie, making talks, raising money for Depression-starved people. His ability and energy fascinated me.

Today he is thought of as a humorist, a wit who commented on national and international affairs. He was far more than that. He was a master of many roles: stage performer, lecturer, movie star, author, newspaper columnist, cowboy, polo player, philosopher, philanthropist, and one of the top proponents of air power and air travel.

He predicted World War II, warning as we built golf courses instead of airports that the Germans would rain bombs on us. He said this on Dec. 7, 1925, fourteen years before World War II started in Europe and sixteen years to the day before the United States was violently thrust into it at Pearl Harbor.

He was a participant in world events, talking with government leaders and influential people all over the globe. He conferred with philosophers, prime ministers, premiers, from Lloyd George in Britain to Mussolini in Italy, to Stalin in the Soviet Union and Irish sage George Bernard Shaw.

He summed up his system this way:

"Most people think I am a gag man. I'm just an ignerant feller, without any education, so to speak, but I try to know what I am talking about. I joke to the public, but I do a lot of studying because, although I hand out a lot of foolishness, I don't want to hand out stuff that might be misleading.

"I read editorials a lot and while I'm reading them, the thought comes to me that I can get this bit of news into the minds of the audience—only in a different way. I have to know what they're talking about to know what's funny. If I was just a clown. . .all those fellows wouldn't take the trouble to explain what they're driving at to me.

"It's a terribly hard job. The guys that tell you they can be funny at any minute, without any effort, are guys that ain't funny to anybody but themselves.

"I depend on the newspapers for most of my inspirations. Some days there is material for several good lines. Then there may be a week when there isn't a little thing worth mentioning. About once a month I turn out a gag that I get a big kick out of myself. That's a pretty good average."

He said that his only set method in "my little gags" was "to try and keep to the truth. Of course you can exaggerate it, but what you say must be based on truth. And I have never found it necessary to use the words 'hell' and 'damn' to get a laugh, either."

He added that he didn't care for jokes that produced the biggest laughs, for they "require no thought at all. I like the one where, if you are with a friend, and hear it, it makes you think; and you nudge your friend and say, 'He's right about that.' I would rather have you do that than to have you laugh—and then forget the next minute what it was you laughed at."

His persona was an ignorant old country boy who didn't know proper spelling or grammar. He was far better educated than he pretended but didn't want to spoil that image by accepting the honorary degrees he was offered.

The gum-chewing cowboy could influence legislation by a quip that was funny and at the same time penetratingly true. He didn't like phonies and had a great knack for getting behind their poses but did it with a disarming grin that took the bitterness from his sallies. With commentary that was never vicious, he made Americans laugh at themselves.

I found only two occasions when Will used so much as a "damn." One involved the Hoover administration's aid to bankers while refusing to feed the hungry. The other involved the apathy of the public.

When *The New York Times* chided him for some of his opinions, he wrote that he was not responsible for the opinions expressed in the *Times* editorial selection, even though its humor was unintentional. But his anger showed through when they questioned his qualifications to comment on world affairs.

He answered that he had been out in the world, talking to people making world decisions, and writers locked in a room in New York were scarcely qualified to evaluate what was going on outside.

Will, who in the early days thought Mussolini was doing a good job in Italy, was later criticized for it. In 1935 he wrote, "I sure would hate to be running for something and have somebody dig back through old papers and confront me with all the nut things that I have shown my ignorance on. You see, conditions and events change so fast, that what is passable today is ridiculous tomorrow."

I have a childhood memory of Will Rogers' smiling face on my mother's bedroom wall. She had lived in Indian Territory, and she considered him a native saint.

"When I'm feeling blue," she'd say, "I can look at the picture of Will and feel better. No matter how bad it gets, he can make you laugh, and somehow your troubles don't seem so bad."

I have another memory of Will Rogers, at Kingsville, Texas, where he used to visit the Klebergs, owners of the famous King Ranch. He greatly admired the Kiñenos, or Mexican-American cowboys, whose families had worked on the ranch for generations. They were fine horsemen, experts at throwing a rope at branding time. Sometimes he went down just to work with them and polish his own remarkable skills with the lasso.

I remember a talk he made at the Forum, a covered patio at Texas A&I College there. All the townspeople gathered to hear him. They weren't disappointed. Although Will was a personal friend of the Kleberg family, he devoted his remarks to making fun of the Klebergs and the ranch.

The family had opposed construction of highways through its vast properties. People didn't dare speak up against the King Ranch in those days. The main industry in town, it controlled the politics.

Will knew this, and he always sided with the little man. He told joke after joke about the highways, with comments the townspeople wished they could say. They laughed until the tears came.

Another memory is a mystery. I can't say with certainty if I saw it or heard about it. I was only six or seven, but the image is so strong my mind has seized the memory as my own.

Will was sitting on the front steps of the corner bank, whittling and thinking. Today such a celebrity would be mobbed by fans wanting at least to shake his hand or ask for an autograph. But he sat there undisturbed. People respected his preoccupation and left him alone with his thoughts.

A final memory of Will Rogers is stamped in my mind—one of those moments you never forget, like where you were and what you were doing when you heard of the Pearl Harbor attack, the assassination of John F. Kennedy, or the Challenger explosion.

I was ten, sitting in my aunt's car outside the Kleberg National Bank in Kingsville when the radio flashed the news that Will Rogers and Wiley Post had been killed in an Alaskan plane crash. It was as if a member of the family had died. The shock and hurt ran deep.

His death, on August 15, 1935, closed down Congress and sent the nation into mourning. The tragedy dominated the news.

Jack Lait wrote, "Of the amazing matters I have covered—crimes, war, disaster—never has any account I have written elicited such a flood of communications from the entire country. . . And not one dissenting word! . . .

Not even the familiar constitutional cranks, carpers and hero-haters have come forward, a unique manifestation."

John McCormack's famous quote summed it up: "A smile has disappeared from the lips of America."

In February, 1929, Will said, "Where does anybody's life come in to be any more valuable than anybody else's? Ain't life just as precious to one as to another? We have heard that 'can't spare you' attitude till we got a lot of men in this country believing it now. Say, get over that old ego. This country will replace you before your folks get home from the funeral."

Will was wrong. He himself was irreplaceable.

A few years ago I began wondering what that rumpled fellow with his wide smile and the hair hanging over his forehead might say if he were around today.

What would he think of our fast-paced, wasteful, high-tech, depersonalized life? And how would generations raised on television and bombarded from birth with vulgar, derisive humor take him?

To paraphrase Texas Sen. Lloyd Bentsen in his campaign debate with Dan Quayle: I'm no Will Rogers.

No one could ever compete with him in style, depth, and class. But I have wanted to recapture some of his spirit in a time when truth and humor are taking a terrible beating.

Hence this book:

All I Know Is What's on TV

—Bill Walraven

On the Media

Will Rogers said:

"Those New York writers should be compelled to get out once in their lifetime and get the 'folks' angle."—December 18, 1932

"The difference between a bandit and a patriot is a good press agent."—March 19, 1932

"You can take a sob story and a stick of candy and lead America right off into the Dead Sea."—December 2, 1923

What Will Might Say Today:
On the Media

It's a great sport these days to stand back and throw mud on a public official, then complain about how dirty he is.

The press can declare a president a failure two weeks before Inauguration Day. Political hacks have the wheels coming off and then wonder why the carriage isn't going anywhere.

People in high places have a hard time defending themselves when accusations and rumors are splashed on the front page but relegated to the burial ground inside if the story turns out to be wrong.

And when the fate of the world is hanging on some great issue, it has a hard time making it to the front page or the top of the newscast, particularly if some celebrity is in sex or crime trouble.

When they stir up a new feeding frenzy, the national press is like a dog chasing its tail while it ignores the horde of fleas and ticks running around on other parts of its anatomy.

Columnists and commentators hold elected officials accountable for all their campaign statements. If we held those talking heads accountable for all the predictions they miss, we'd find out who the real experts are.

C-SPAN brings us meetings, congressional sessions, and speeches, as they happen, without comment. The networks and news services must send their reporters to a different planet. Sometimes we can't even recognize those events when we see how they show up on the evening news or in the morning paper.

Where there's trouble, you'll find TV cameras. Or reverse that. Where there's TV cameras, you'll find trouble. When the TV cameras leave, the troublemakers go home.

We Americans have learned not to worry because we've convinced ourselves that newscasts are just another TV show. Nothing is really that bad. The pain and agony aren't real. And even when the scenes catch our attention, before long we get used to them. After a few weeks, they're just more reruns.

Newspapers and television have become big business, concentrated in fewer and fewer hands. Editorial decisions used to be made in the newsroom. Today too many are made in the business office.

If you can't get a ticket to a talk show, stick around. Maybe they'll let you start a show of your own.

Pretty women can tell a TV audience how to conduct a happy married life even if they've been married three or four times. They're like the stubborn old farmer who said, "You can't teach me nuthin' about farming. Why, I've worn out four farms in my day."

When we had the old-fashioned party-line telephones, people all along the way listened in to catch up on the latest gossip. Sometimes so many tuned in they drained the phone lines of electricity.

Then technology brought us private lines. But now they're so technical that snoopers are listening in on the secret conversations of princes and presidents and then broadcasting their most private statements.

So when you're on the line, there could be quite a few parties out there listening in. If you have something spicy you don't want the world to know about, better keep it to yourself or you'll likely end up in the tabloids, right alongside Prince Charles.

We're hard on dope addicts, but we're all addicted to something, whether it's coffee, beer, whiskey, chewing gum, guns, hunting, fishing, golf, bridge, or driving a car as fast as it will go. But the biggest addiction of all cuts off all serious talk. It takes up time you could spend doing something you'll remember an hour later. It's called television.

Now, radio and television are wonderful sales devices. They've always done a good job of selling beer and soap powder. Today they push everything from political ideas to talk-show hosts.

Unfortunately, the hottest merchandise around is

hate. Hate may get a lot of laughs, but that doesn't make it funny.

Some of Rush Limbaugh's worshipers call him the "Will Rogers of the 90s." But Will spoke to the decency of the common man, while Rush speaks to the unspeakable. When it comes to comparing him to Will Rogers, Rush would be better described as the "mirror image."

'I dunno, boss. I just don't think you'll ever fill 'em.'

Television wants to know what's going on right now. If you don't know, you're holding out. If you won't say, you're part of a conspiracy.

If a plane crashes, reporters are on the scene before any investigation, getting opinions on what caused the disaster.

They don't necessarily want the truth. They want an answer— now. By tomorrow they'll want answers to something else nobody has had time to figure out. And they'll find a quote and a sound bite, even if they have to pay an "expert" for it.

The mission of too much of the media is to make sure government doesn't work. They criticize everything suggested to solve any problem, but they never seem to come up with what's right with the world or what it will take to cure its ills.

What we need in the press is more carpenters and fewer demolition experts.

But then, slandering our presidents has always been a popular pastime. Critics said George Washington wore wooden teeth, snickered about Thomas Jefferson's attention to a female slave, gossiped that Rachel Donelson wasn't divorced when she married Andrew Jackson. They called Lincoln an ape, Grant a drunkard, and Franklin Pierce a coward because he fell down during a charge in the Mexican War.

They wrote about Grover Cleveland's illegitimate child and Warren G. Harding's peccadilloes. They laughed at Gerald Ford for clumsy stumbling and Jimmy Carter for being attacked by a rabbit.

Media folk were tolerant of sexual escapades of Franklin D. Roosevelt, Dwight Eisenhower, and John F.

Kennedy.

But TV is so pushy and eats up material in such big gulps that anything is fair game now. And when those magazine and television editors get through doctoring pictures with their computers, there's no telling what we'll see.

On Crime

Will Rogers said:

"If there be one thing that has increased crime, it's been the Automatic Pistol. It's made no practice necessary to be an outlaw. Give any young Egotist two shots of dope and an Automatic and he will hold up the Government Mint."—June 7, 1931

"I havent got sense enough to know whether our criminal court procedure is brokendown, or lame, or limping, or whatever . . . but something sure is cuckoo when it takes . . . all this time to convict one after he has confessed. It looks like after a person's guilt in this country is established, why then the battle as to whether he should be punished is the real test of the court."—February 26, 1928

"We don't give our criminals much punishment, but we sure give 'em plenty of publicity."—February 2, 1934

What Will Might Say Today:
On Crime

Strange as it may seem, some of our best police officers are dogs. They sniff out more crimes, make more "collars," work for just a few words of praise, and never ask for a uniform allowance.

It used to be you sent your clothes to the laundry and put your money in the bank. Now people send their money to the bank to be laundered so they'll be able to get their $1,000 suits cleaned.

We don't really need a bunch of new prisons to house all the criminals. Just lock up the people and let the criminals have the rest of the country.

Or we could just turn all of the thugs loose in Washington City. It would serve them right—might scare them into going straight.

If you're going to commit a sensational crime, first make sure you have a good agent to handle the book, TV, and movie rights. The movie may come out before the jury is selected, and potential jurors can choose from half a dozen books telling how guilty or innocent you are.

We've decided a pound of cure is worth an ounce of prevention. We'd rather pay medical bills than keep people from getting sick. We'd rather build prisons than start kids off straight. We're so used to installment buying, we've forgotten the benefits of paying up front.

There was a time when teenage capers were called childish pranks. Those pranks have grown to drive-by shootings, carjacking, robbery, dope dealing, rape, murder—you name it.

Juveniles have earned the full rights of the adult criminal to serve penitentiary time and, sadly, the right to be executed. Not only have they bridged the gap between childhood and adulthood—they've burned it behind them.

Drugs are an important part of our economy—we're the biggest marketplace in the world.

If it wasn't for drugs, seventy-five percent of our criminals would starve to death.

It doesn't seem like we learned anything from prohibition. When booze was illegal, Americans crowded into speakeasies to soak up the stuff.

We created a new class of gangster that became the Mafia—crime barons and gangsters who cruised the streets, guns blazing. The government spent billions on ineffective enforcement, and people seemed encouraged by the challenge.

Now, with illegal drugs so profitable, we're creating killer billionaires and a new class of organized mobsters who control our lives. We have international gangs, national gangs, and neighborhood gangs.

Make anything valuable enough, everybody will want it, no matter what the cost.

Everything is a conspiracy. They say there was one in President Lincoln's assassination and others in the deaths of John F. Kennedy, Robert Kennedy, and Martin Luther King, Jr. Any time there's a murder involving a prominent person, they—lawyers are good at this—see dark, sinister plots.

We could save a lot of time by dispensing with the murder trials and getting right on to the conspiracies.

It's an established fact that the more you steal, the less the punishment. The champion thieves, at worst, get sent to country club prisons. Usually they get probation, or maybe some time in public service, while small-time crooks spend many years making license plates.

A Wall Street thief who stole millions and millions from investors and helped bring down the savings and loans was soaked good. They didn't want to be too rough on him so they let him keep $125 million plus a few perks.

If he had stolen a few hundred, he'd still be working in the prison laundry.

It pays to think big.

Almost everyone has civil rights except police officers. If they're charged with an offense but found innocent, the prosecutors find a way to try them all over again in a different jurisdiction. The average criminal is home free after a not-guilty verdict.

With so many states okaying concealed weapons, the Old West is coming back. The shooter can always say, "I thought he was going for his gun."

And some thugs claim self-defense when they shoot a policeman. After all, the cop was wearing a pistol, so the "victim" feared for his life.

'Yo, it was self-defense. He was packin' a *gun*, man!'

It would seem that everybody in this country has the constitutional right to kill somebody, just so long as he or she does the job cleanly with a pistol or rifle. Shotguns and knives are crude tools to use in committing mayhem—almost un-American.

It's OK for defense lawyers to destroy the credibility of witnesses in a criminal case by ruining their reputations and sometimes their lives.

But sometimes the prosecution can't tell the jury that the nice young fellow sitting there with a fresh haircut and new suit is actually a dirty murdering thug with a prison record as long as your arm.

It's strange. We have more freedom than anybody. And we lock up a greater percentage of our population than any other country on the face of the earth. Our prisons are so crowded we have to release an inmate when we lock up another one. Yet Republicans call it pork when somebody suggests spending money to keep people from doing crimes.

The money they aren't spending will go for more prisons. And we won't have any trouble filling them up.

On Lawyers

Will Rogers said:

"I have always noticed that anytime a man can't come and settle with you without bringing his lawyer, why look out for him."—January 14, 1923

"Just think, America has one hundred and ten million population, 90 percent of which are Lawyers, yet we can't find two of them who have not worked at some time or another for an oil company."—1924

"Thirty-five hundred lawyers of the American Bar Association are here eating us out of house and home. They are here, they say, 'to preserve the Constitution. . . .' What they ought to be here for and that would make this convention immortal, is to kick the crooks out of their profession, they should recommend a law that in every case that went on trial, the defending lawyer should be tried first. Then if he comes clear, he would be eligible to defend. As it is now, they are trying the wrong man."—July 14, 1935

What Will Might Say Today:
On Lawyers

A recent survey showed there are almost as many lawyers as there are cockroaches. And we'll never get rid of either one of them.

Maybe there ought to be some sort of birth control device for lawyers, preferably retroactive.

At the present rate of growth, there will eventually be one lawyer for every citizen. If they don't start drowning babies who plan to become lawyers, America's going to be a land named Sue.

Lawyers like to legislate loopholes so other lawyers can beat the laws and file more lawsuits. No wonder teachers nowadays can't discipline without being sued, doctors can't operate without looking over their shoulders, and police don't dare pull their pistols.

With help from television, juicy trials have replaced the circus as the greatest show on earth.

There may be a solution to this deficit thing. If we put a surtax on lawyers, we'd be out of the woods in no time. But, on the other hand, who'd say "Sir" to a lawyer?

A lawyer out in California has found a gold mine suing other lawyers. That's the greatest thing since fried okra. That fella figured out where the money is.

No need for rules in sports anymore—we have lawyers.

You'll have to admit the lawyers are doing their part

to keep people out of jail, particularly if they have money.

Prosecutors have a great way to improve their averages. When two crooks are arrested, the prosecutor tells one of them he can take a walk if he'll help get his partner a job in the license plate factory. That way we cut down the prison population by following a proven marketing trick: Buy one and get one free.

Every time we put a prisoner in the front door, we have to let another one out the back door, no matter how many new prisons we build. Some occupants of that valuable space have been there ten years or more in the most expensive seats in the house—those on death row.

They're waiting on their latest appeal. This provides the legal profession with a reliable pension, often at the expense of those who live outside the walls.

Some of the most active lawyers in the country are amateur lawyers serving time in penitentiaries. They spend most of their time in prison libraries thinking up new ways to gum up the judicial system by filing nuisance lawsuits. One such suit was a prisoner's complaint that he had to eat crunchy peanut butter when he wanted the smooth kind.

If you think this is nutty, they actually collect on some of these cases.

Used to, juries dispensed justice by determining which lawyer had a snotty attitude, which one seemed sneaky, which one was mean to witnesses, or which one shouted and scared the jurors into thinking they were about to go to hell.

Now the lawyers use psychologists and their computers to prepackage the jury so they know the verdict before the testimony begins.

Of course, one thing that sticks in the mind of the jury is what was said just before the judge said: "The jury is instructed to disregard the remarks of counsel."

Without a courtroom program, you can still tell the plaintiff—he's the fellow who is shouting and angry. The defendant is the guy with the hurt look in his eyes, and the judge is the one in the high seat asleep.

Our judicial system has become such a patchwork of rulings on top of rulings that lawyers can peel anything they want to off it.

For one thing, we have to give the masses who graduate from law school every year something to do to keep them from going on welfare.

I guess the system could be simplified, but if IRS forms are any guide, we should probably leave it alone.

On Politics

Will Rogers said:

"I bet you have had Political enemies and you would think from your impressions of them that they ought to be quartered in the zoo in the reptile house. Yet when you met them you could see their side and find they wasent so bad, and that you were both trying to get about the same thing in the long run."—1927

"Papers say, 'what would Lincoln do today?' Well, in the first place he wouldn't chop any wood. He would trade in his ax on a Ford. Being a Republican, he would vote the Democratic ticket. Being in sympathy for the underdog, he would be classed as a radical progressive. Having a sense of humor, he would be called eccentric."—February 12, 1934

"Party politics is the most narrow-minded occupation in the world. A guy raised in a straight jacket is a corkscrew compared to a thick headed party politician. All you would have to do to make some men atheists is just tell them the Lord belonged to the opposition party. After that they could never see any good in Him."—March 29, 1925

What Will Might Say Today:
On Politics

There seems to be more radicals than ever around these days. Radical is what a nut on the far side of a political issue thinks about the nuts on the other far side of the same issue.

When it comes time to choose our presidential candidates, we let farmers in Iowa and rock-ribbed New Englanders in New Hampshire have a head start. Hawaii should hold primaries in early January. I don't know how that would affect the electoral system, but it would be a lot more comfortable for the candidates and hordes of reporters,photographers, and commentators who traipse after them.

Candidates and contributors are caught up in a system of mutual chicanery.
Successful politicians are elected by special interests, kept in office by payoffs, rewarded by kickbacks, and presented suitcases filled with money for uttering words some hack of a former newspaperman wrote.
Then we call them "incumbent." That sounds a lot better than "scoundrel."

In Mexico paying bribes to get government action is called *mordida*. In the good ol' USA it's called "campaign contributions."

A lot of people don't want to run for office. They don't want to get beat up for going out and talking about issues and telling the truth.

Those are the folks we need to get out and campaign and tell us what's going on.

They'll get beat, but they'll serve a wonderful patriotic duty.

The average politician's idea of a news conference is one question answered by a half-hour speech.

The outcome of future presidential races will be determined by whose computer breaks down first. Being a smart fellow who can get things done doesn't count. It's having good spin doctors and a computer dossier of every living American and a few dead ones.

What's a "spin doctor"? We used to call them press agents. They're the people who take what's happened and spin it around until you can't tell straight up from the truth of the matter.

If you went around making extravagant claims that advertisers make, you'd be branded a mud brain, a liar, and just a little bit of a thief. Yet we swallow all the hogwash the flacks dish out.

So when the politicians come along and make claims we know they can't back up, we naturally elect them anyway. It's kind of like buying a used car.

TV people who use a teleprompter to read news reports other people have researched and written call themselves "anchors." The same thing sometimes happens in Washington, when speech writers feed words into the prompter and the speaker who gets credit for it is called "Mr. President."

The politician isn't a person. He's a prerecorded message, a television rerun, a sound bite, a photo op. He's whatever his teleprompter says he is. He's an automat who minds his handlers—the modern political machine.

And if the power fails, he might just disappear in a "pouf."

'See! I *told* you he was all smoke n' mirrors.'

We spend more time looking into politicians' bedrooms than we do looking into their brains. It's getting to where the only presidents who can have sex are the dead ones.

Presidents need friends real bad. What they don't need is relatives.

Political polling is like having somebody take your temperature every few hours until you're convinced you really are sick. All the heat is in the hands of the nurse holding the thermometer.

The barkeep at the pub near Oxford University said proudly, "This is the very spot where your President Clinton drank his beer when he was a student here."

"Surely he wouldn't do a thing like that," an American tourist joked.

"Yes," the pub keeper answered, "but he didn't swallow it."

Democrats blame the Republicans for depressions. Republicans blame the Democrats for wars. It makes you depressed and ready to fight to listen to either one of them.

And both parties blame the other for the budget deficit. Republicans say Democrats caused it with wasteful welfare spending. Democrats claim Republicans caused it with wasteful defense spending. They're probably both right.

The Republicans had the presidency and the veto. The Democrats had the Congress and couldn't pass anything. Next the Democrats got the presidency, and Congress still didn't do much. Then the Republicans took over with their "Contract for

America."

But it didn't take long for folks to start calling it the "Contract on America."

After their "First Hundred Days," the Republicans celebrated their contract by bringing a circus to town. They had elephants and everything, right outside the Capitol.

But they really didn't need to recruit any clowns. They had enough clowns in the House of Representatives.

For years they said the South will rise again. In the election of '94, it did. With head Rebel Newt Gingrich in charge, the Republicans started to thump the tub for States Rights. Makes you wonder what else they might try to bring back from the Old Confederacy.

Poisoned water, dead forests, acid rain, falling bridges, raw sewage—these don't worry the GOP. The problem is, the Republicans had been passengers so long they forgot how to drive.

Whoever said "Nice guys finish last" knew what he was talking about. If you go to the people and tell them what you'd like to do, you're a liar when you can't carry out all your plans.

But if you campaign by tearing down your opponents, calling them scoundrels and thieves and accusing them of all kinds of crimes, you'll probably win.

These days the most successful candidates wrap themselves in the American flag and throw rocks at the government.

A good way to handle presidential candidates is to turn off the sound. It would be an even better test to turn off the teleprompters.

But there's one good thing about presidential elections—
they make it easy to kick the TV habit.

Politics is just like the Super Bowl. Winning isn't the most
important thing—it's the only thing. No matter what you've done,
if you're No. 2, you're a loser.

What the president or Congress does or tries to accomplish
is irrelevant. All that counts is how whatever happens will affect
the next election.

Ol' Abe Lincoln had less than forty percent of the popular
vote, and he made a fair to middlin' president.

Would ugly old Abe with his high-pitched voice have a
chance on TV? Or 300-lb. William Howard Taft? Or Franklin D.
Roosevelt with his shriveled legs?

We used to choose a president for his stand on the issues.
Now he needs a good voice, pretty hair, and white teeth. But the
most important qualification is millions of dollars in his campaign
treasury.

And if Abe was around today, he'd have to revise his thinking. Because of television, politicians can fool most of the
people nearly all of the time.

On Government

Will Rogers said:

"On account of us being a democracy and run by the people, we are the only nation in the world that has to keep a government four years, no matter what it does."—December 22, 1929

". . . everybody is on a trip somewhere if they work for the Government. I wonder when the taxpayers take their trip."—July 8, 1923

"Al Smith told exactly what his ideas were on every important question. No wonder he dant get elected. Imagine a man in public office that everbody knew where he stood. We wouldn't call him a statesman, we would call him a curiosity."—March 1, 1933

What Will Might Say Today:
On Government

Taking government controls from the banks and savings and loans was like taking down the fence and letting the hogs into the corn, then complaining because there wasn't any corn for people to eat. Ever try to tell a hog to quit eating?

The Savings and Loan mess taught us one lesson—we're slow learners. Politicians from both parties decided money lenders didn't have to go by the rules, and a lot of people didn't care if those money lenders stole their money. After all, it was insured. But the insurance company was us—the U.S. government—so it ended up costing every man, woman, and child in the country several thousand dollars.

At the same time they were taking the controls off, Congress and the president decided to save money by firing a bunch of the investigators who were supposed to catch the thieves.

Still, nobody's very worried. The bill isn't due—yet. But if the tax collector came to pick up the S&L money from every family instead of stacking it on the national debt, a lot more bankers and money changers would be in hot water.

We'll all appreciate the Savings and Loan debts

when Uncle Sam tells us he wants his $5,000 from each of us and each of our children. Then we'll understand the lesson of the S&L scandal.

Democrats blame former President Reagan for relaxing the Savings and Loan rules and taking the locks off the doors. Republicans say Congress did it. If you could go to jail for finger-pointing, there wouldn't be many people left in Washington.

Politicians were pretty slick when they got the income tax on the really rich cut from seventy percent to thirty. This made people with a lot of money real happy. Raising Social Security taxes helped make up the difference. And all the money spent on tanks and aircraft carriers provided a bunch of jobs.

Everybody felt good.

Now the interest payment amounts to a third of everything the government spends, and a lot of us don't feel so good any more. Reckon the way out of the mess is to cut the rich guy's taxes some more?

Americans are a peculiar breed. They demand that crooks be sent to jail, but they don't want to pay taxes to build prisons. Still, if we could keep from convicting government officials for high crimes, the prisons wouldn't be so crowded.

Excess government spending is money Congress votes for some other class of people.

Bureaucrats are pretty smart. They built big housing projects for poor people who couldn't afford houses. That way, they confined a lot of the violence and crime to one place in hopes it won't break out to bother the rest of us.

At one time you had to pay a poll tax in order to vote. That was unconstitutional. Then the courts decided that some voters need help because they don't vote. Those folks sued, and out of the suits came single-member voting districts.

When Boss Tweed was around, they called that the ward system. That was bad. It was more honest to elect politicians at large.

Now at-large elections are bad. Single-member districts help candidates get elected even though not many people want to vote for them.

As soon as they learn how to steal public money, hire ward heelers, and kick back some patronage to the folks down the block for their vote, they'll earn the privilege of being called "Boss."

Then the system will be unpopular all over again.

Every time the government goes to reform something, they try to fix it by turning it over to the bureau that messed it up to start with.

That's like paying the kid who busted out the windowpane to put another one in.

Or they create a new agency to solve the problem. But that makes the problem bigger, because the agency has to keep the problem going to justify their job.

There's a tendency for government to get out of the service business. They farm out prisons, utilities, and

garbage collection. They turn their agencies into businesses. That's called "privatizing."

Privatizing may be great for the business, as long as
it doesn't go bankrupt, but Army recruits have never
cared much for it. Private's not a position to aspire to.

But when it comes to cutting down on the bureau-
cracy, the Republicans don't worry about throwing the
baby out with the bath water. They'll just send the baby
out to a commercial car wash.

The government prints all kinds of pretty postage
stamps and sells them to collectors. The stamps get
more valuable with time.

Now, if the government could just print a bunch of
different kinds of greenbacks which would get more
valuable tucked away under the socks, people wouldn't
have to worry about the interest rates they'll get from
their bank or credit union.

A poor feller who shoplifts a turnip from the store will
have all kinds of trouble making bail. But when a banker
goes broke, the government bails him out.

That takes some mighty big buckets to get him back
afloat. And the taxpayers have to bail a little faster to fill
the buckets.

President Grover Cleveland would have the devil's
own time getting elected today. He admitted he'd fathered
an illegitimate child and was paying support for it. The
straitlaced Victorians of the 1880s considered his public
record more important than his private life.

But today, when the country has the morals of a street cur, we demand that our public officials be pure as the driven snow.

We want our presidents to be perfect. If we applied these same standards to star entertainers and professional athletes, they'd have to go to work for a living.

America has seen some turnarounds. When the moguls learned they could profit from a big national debt, we changed from anti- to pro- on deficit spending. We also changed from isolationist to arms supplier. The problem with that is you never know when the other guys will quit shooting each other and point the guns at us.

Every circus needs its clowns. As a country we are lucky to have the CIA. The trouble is, they don't intend to be clowns. It just works out that way.

How else could they give people bombs and teach them how to throw them, then have to duck as they throw them at us?

We only hear about the CIA when it goofs up. That's why it really isn't a secret organization.

Aldrich Hazen Ames, one of our CIA spooks, took money from the Russians and gave information that got a bunch of agents killed. He picked a good place to hide. Nobody thought of looking for a Russian spy in the agency itself.

And only in our nation's capital could a governmental agency spend hundreds of millions of dollars building a palace and nobody know what it's to be used for or who's paying for it.

It was news to the White House. It was news to

Congress. But the CIA knew about it. It was a building for the intelligence community.

After hearing about Ames, it makes you wonder if the KGB will have an office in that building.

'. . . Who *is* that guy?'

There's supposed to be three branches of government, the Executive, the Legislative, and the Judicial. But actually there are four, and the fourth could be the most powerful of all—the Lobbies.

It doesn't depend on voters. It's supported by dollars. You might say the Greenback Party has returned.

For years it's been a custom to appoint rich party contributors to plush jobs as ambassador to France, Greece, Britain, or some other place that recognizes richness as a form of diplomacy. In effect, these posts go to the highest bidder.

We could solve some of our problems by filling seats in Congress with people who were smart enough to have very rich parents. They could bid millions more than the present officeholders are being bought for, and the money could be used against the national debt.

Furthermore, the president's job should be limited to candidates who are at least billionaires willing to further enrich the treasury. The vice presidency could go for multi-millions. The government we have now, bought and paid for by lobbyists, would be obsolete.

There'd be no need for long campaigns and wasteful political conventions. But Washington cocktail parties wouldn't be nearly so interesting.

If you're rich, you get a subsidy. If you're poor, it's welfare. The pay's better from subsidies.

The states are outdoing each other in raising money by gambling. They have lotteries. Some are setting up football betting parlors and raking in the money from roulette and blackjack tables, and a lot of gambling professionals are going hungry.

What if the government went into the burglary, strong arm, and murder business? Would nationalizing crime put the criminals out of work?

Uncle Sam doesn't play fair. If you don't pay your taxes ahead of time, he'll fine the dickens out of you, yet he doesn't plan to pay his debts until from now till Kingdom Come.

Government is an illusion. A leader doesn't have to accomplish anything. He calls a press conference and tells everybody what he has done. It really doesn't get done, but who cares, so long as everyone thinks he's done something.

Call a press conference, and the drug problem is solved. Call another one, the education problem is solved. If we have enough press conferences, we won't have a worry in the world.

We've managed to keep our scientists busy during slack employment periods. We've spent billions having them design interstellar space projects. We've had them dig big tunnels in the earth for a great big superconducting super collider to probe the innermost secrets of the universe. Then we cancel the projects.

Fortunately, the scientists can find another job. I don't know where they'll fit in in outer space, but they can always work on the mushroom farm they're planning in the fourteen miles of tunnel at Waxahachie, Texas.

See if this makes sense:

The government wants people to quit smoking but gives money to farmers to raise tobacco.

They've got the air-conditioner and furnace both running at the same time.

Government is no longer controlled by political parties. In 1992 Bill Clinton was elected with the help of many of the same moneybags who gave to Republicans.

No special interest can afford to be left out, so they hedge by giving to both sides. Parties don't count. Money does.

Washington has the answer to nearly every problem. If people are starving, quit feeding them and they'll disappear.

The next best thing is the block grant. Send the money down to the local level. By the time they get through fighting over it in the State House, the Courthouse, and the City Hall, there won't be anything left in the bucket.

And every time they let the states pick up the tab, it lets the feds off the hook and points the outrage at the governors and the mayors.

It's an axiom with income taxes — the less you need a refund, the more you'll get back.

Taxes has become such a hated word we think gambling is better. Pretty soon, when people need a cop, they'll have to buy a lottery ticket and hope they win.

We used to leave foreign policy to our Secretaries of State. They managed to get us in a heap of trouble. But foreign policy determined by opinion polls is an even worse idea. When polls are published about what the average Americans know, sixty percent can't tell who Mickey Mouse is.

The bureaucrats get a lot of bad press, but thousands of workers dedicate their lives to government service with little credit.

They're like everyone else. Nobody pays any attention to them when they're working hard and behaving themselves.

I've been asked, "Have you ever known the government to do anything right?"

Actually, there's a lot more right with the government than most folks give it credit for.

A lot of those critics went to college on the GI Bill. Now they get Social Security. They're on Medicare, their kids got student loans, and their savings are insured by the FDIC. They drive on interstate highways, and they want a big Army, Air Force, and Navy to keep their bases open.

No one notices when the water is pure, the mail comes on time, the garbage gets picked up, and the crime rate goes down. It's easier to complain when something is wrong.

You don't pay much attention to the electric company until it turns your power off. Same way with the government. You won't appreciate its services until they're gone.

And before we criticize, we should look in the mirror and see who dealt us this mess.

On Education

Will Rogers said:

"The football season is about over. Education never had a more financial year. School will start now."—November 20, 1927

"Our children are delivered to the Schools in Automobiles. But whether that adds to their grades is doubtful. There hasent been a Thomas Jefferson produced in this country since we formed our first Trust . . . There hasent been a Patrick Henry showed up since business men quit eating lunch with their families, joined a club and have indigestion from amateur Oratory."—June 2, 1928

"Its funny how quick a college boy can find out that the world is wrong. . . let him go to college and he will be the first on the square on May Day to shout down with the government."—March 29, 1931

What Will Might Say Today:
On Education

Sometimes you have to hit a mule right between the eyes to get his attention. Did kids quit paying attention in school when lawyers forced teachers to put away the paddle? The seat of the pants might not be the seat of learning, but it used to be a real good attention getter.

Of course, today this is a country which doesn't think kids should be spanked. Do you think if they paddled the teachers, kids would pay attention?

Education used to focus on the Three R's — readin', 'ritin', and 'rithmetic. Now it's the Three T's: television, tuition, and tests.

Our schools have been turning out students who can't read.

If a factory turned out lawn mowers with no blades, the stockholders would have the plant manager, the board of directors, and the president of the board mopping floors or drummed out of the corporation.

A lot of educationalists seem to know about all there is to know except how to teach. They keep replacing one theory that doesn't work with another that doesn't work any better. Thinking up new ideas gives them big pay-checks, while the kids learn less and less.

Maybe we should go back to the future. One teacher I know used phonics flashcards to help her pupils learn. Then she found some cards just like them in her great-grandfather's attic. Instead of building new schools, we might try those of the 1890s.

All of which makes you wonder if our ancestors were smarter than we are. They sat there on hard benches in a drafty classroom with all the other classes and killed time by learning Latin and Greek. Somewhere along the line they learned to read, write, and speak fluent English. They had more sense than to sit in an air-conditioned classroom, yawning from watching the late-late show and waiting for the teacher to get caught up on her paper-work.

Professors used to profess in front of a class. Now they profess in books and research projects, and students seldom see them.

The daddies and mommies probably don't know this, since they selected the university for all the high-sounding names on the brochures. But their money helps pay the big salaries the professors need to keep up their book promotions.

There's quite a fuss about prayer in the schools. School prayer, like flag burning or invading a Caribbean island or two, takes center stage when there's a need to distract attention from some major problem that's about to bust out.

There's nothing wrong with allowing a student to have a moment of silent meditation, as long as he doesn't take it just when the teacher asks him a question.

But pupils should be limited as to the amount of time they spend at silent prayer or they might escape into a nap.

'He's been deep in prayer for over an hour.'

There's no law saying you can't close your eyes and say a silent prayer anywhere you want to. Some people don't want to pray unless they have a loudspeaker.

The schools of education are run by some pretty peculiar specimens. They've convinced us to spend most of our money on the D and F students and let the bright kids take care of themselves. We're getting ourselves in a pickle—we need the smart people. You don't run mules in the Kentucky Derby.

Many years ago radio comedian Fred Allen said of TV at its start, "Kids are going to have eyeballs as big as saucers and no brains at all."
Was he right?
Check out the test scores.

On the Day's World

Will Rogers said:

"I am not the fellow to go to a Country and then start criticizing it from our angle at home. You have to look at a thing through their eyes to be fair."—1926

"I stood in the Roman Forum and I found out they had a Senate in Rome long ago. That's why Rome declined. Boy! If they declined with a Senate, what will we do with a Senate and a House."— June 1926

"Their (European) diplomats are trained. It's their life business. Ours makes a campaign contribution and wakes up in Belgium and don't know which ocean he crossed to get there." —March 16, 1935

What Will Might Say Today:

On the Day's World

Cubans, Vietnamese, Mexicans, Chinese—all want in. So many have come that even the Lady of Liberty is getting tired.

But it's amazing how many of these newcomers are willing to roll up their sleeves and get some dirt under their fingernails.

Before World War II the Japanese came over and bought up our scrap metal, then dropped it on our boys as bombs. After the war, Japan took our metal and dropped it on us as Toyotas and Hondas.

The Japanese relaxed their import policy for United States beef. At the same time there was a great increase in the purchase of ranches in this country by Japanese.

You'll know this is true when you see Oriental cowboys massaging tough old steers to tenderize the beef on the hoof. And rodeos will be a little different, too, when they serve raw fish in the stands.

They say if you put oil on troubled waters, things will calm down. But it's the oil under the waters, and deserts, too, that makes us send our bombers and tanks in to make peace.

We don't want to bother with trouble spots that have nothing but poor folks as their primary resource.

It was natural we had to rescue the poor Emir of Kuwait. We weren't really interested in saving the bacon of a ruler who had virgins supplied to him on a weekly basis, but we were pained to see Saddam Hussein grabbing off the cheap oil we'd been buying.

Other poor souls living under a tyrant's heel are just going to have to do some wildcatting and get our attention with oil to stir up some righteous outrage.

Lots of people in the city never get to know the people living across the street. Now folks out on the farm are having the same trouble.

At one time they stopped in to sit a spell with the neighbor down the road. Now it's not so easy to visit, being as how the neighbor lives in a skyscraper in downtown Tokyo or Bonn.

Uncle Sam is doing an awful lot for the poor farmers in the developing nations. We provide markets for their poppy plants, their coca plants, and their cannibis. That way we've lowered their taxes and created some of the richest mobsters in the world.

It's not a good idea to make a trade with a terrorist. If he has a hostage, he'll keep the hostage, your gun, and your money, and put a bomb in your pocket on the way out.

One way to tell terrorists from patriots is to find out who they've attacked.

It's hard to threaten a terrorist. What do you tell a zealot who's going to blow himself up, "Stop that, fella, or I'll shoot"?

Try going to the bank and asking for a big loan. They'll want your house, your car, and your mother-in-law as collateral. Developing nations have got billions with no collateral at all. They might be underdeveloped, but they sure aren't dumb.

When the dollar goes up, we go to Europe and Japan. When it goes down, the Europeans and the Japanese come over here.

And when the peso goes down, nearly everybody in Mexico becomes a tourist in this country.

But don't make fun of Mexico for being a poor nation. We owe a lot more than they do.

You can tell those Americans who've been to Europe. They'll put a little mark across their sevens. Europeans do that because otherwise their sevens and twos would look alike.

And if someone holds his fork prongs down in his hand, eats with his left hand, and never lets go of his knife, he's probably a world traveler showing off.

They say the European grasp on the knife is a holdover from the days of knights, when they kept their swords close at hand. More likely they need the knife as a shovel, since they don't give you bread in restaurants over there.

Every time we try to break up a fight, we get a black eye. If you step into the middle of a family brouhaha, both sides will turn on you. People who've been fighting for a thousand years aren't likely to listen to some outsider.

When one of our fellow countries is having a family squabble, we should first pick the side we think we ought to be on, then change sides.

We never seem to choose the right one the first time.

In China and Cuba they still talk Marxism, but they're turning to capitalism. Seems it helps them eat better.

You really must feel sorry for the Cubans. They have the best cigars in the world. But they don't have a decent dinner to smoke them after.

It's scary watching the Russians playing around with democracy at home. They're just trying to ruin our economy by forcing us to quit building war machines.

Russia's democracy will start to work when they realize you really can get paid if you work at it. And some day the stores will sell stuff they can afford.

The Russians have never had any practice at democracy. They didn't get much help from us, but they're catching up. They have a rising crime rate. Homeless people crowd the railroad stations.

Gangs are a problem. Politicians are screaming at each other. Yes, they're definitely making progress.

On the Military

Will Rogers said:

"Every time we start on a humanitarian mission, we come back with both legs in a sling."—1926

"There is only one unpardonable thing you can talk about in the Navy, Army or in politics, and that is to propose to cut down the expenditure. You can accuse them of negligence and even laziness, but to suggest spending less money?"

"You can't say civilization don't advance, however, for in every war they kill you in a new way."—December 22, 1929

What Will Might Say Today:
On the Military

Citizens everywhere applaud the government
saving money by closing obsolete military
bases. That means bases on the other side of the country.

Military brass always want to fight the next war with
the weapons and tactics of the last one. What a trick it
would be to get both sides to go back to bows and ar-
rows.

We'll have to be careful if presidents start little wars
to stay in office. Pretty soon we might be afraid to hold
elections.

Generals aren't a very good source for news, if you
really want to know what's going on.
But it shouldn't be unpatriotic to tell the truth.

In a modern invasion, the biggest obstacle isn't the
enemy. It's the waves of newspeople waiting there to
meet our troops when they land.

'Any sign that you've been spotted?'

If they really want to solve the budget problem, they should make a rule that nobody in a defense industry who held a military rank higher than second lieutenant or ensign can do business with the Defense Department after they retire.

The influence of former generals and admirals runs up the cost a billion here and a billion there. Pretty soon, like the fella said, it starts to get expensive.

It was a real comfort to know we had weapons that could kill a Russian 2,500 times while he was killing us only 400 times.

Now the problem we both have with those weapons is not where to use them but how to get rid of them.

We Americans are afraid of being called second-rate, so we cheer every time we whip up on some third-rate country. We don't want to admit it, but that's the stuff bullies are made of.

And when we win a piddlin' little war, we do an awful lot of celebrating. After Desert Storm, we spent almost as much on parades as we did for the fighting.

Clinical bombing (you don't see the blood), collateral damage (dead civilians we don't want to talk about), friendly fire (our people killed by our own weapons)—if we invent enough fancy words, we can make war a video game.

Despite the parades, martial music, the flags and the cheering, there's no such thing as a good war. We make a big mistake when we confuse war and the Super Bowl.

But when we send our military to do a job, we shouldn't demand they be brought home at the first sign of combat or casualties. That gives troublemakers in other hot spots the idea that our colors will run.

That's not fair to our armed forces.

They're trained to fight. They have the courage and will, but their mission becomes impossible when TV cameras zoom in on every skirmish, critics second guess every move, and politicians won't support the commander-in-chief unless he's in the right political party.

Sure, it IS a terrible sight when television brings a war right into our living rooms. If they'd had TV crews at Valley Forge or Gettysburg or Pearl Harbor, no telling where we'd be today.

On the Economy

Will Rogers said:

"When everybody has got money, they cut taxes and when they're broke, they raise 'em."
—March 14, 1932

"No nation in the history of the world was ever sitting as pretty. If we want anything, all we have to do is go and buy it on credit. So that leaves us without any economic problems whatsoever, except perhaps some day to have to pay for them."

"An economist is a man who can tell you what can happen under any given conditions, and his guess is liable to be just as good as anybody else's."—May 26, 1935

What Will Might Say Today:

On the Economy

Economics is really very simple. The government and most of the people are spending more than they earn. The solution is to take the credit cards away from both the people and the government.

Did you ever stop to think that right now might be the good ol' days? Our great-grandchildren will wish they could have lived back when both the people and the government were credit-card rich.

You've got to feel sorry for the little babies being born. Already they owe more than their grandpas made in a lifetime.

With new technology, it's possible to have your photograph engraved on your granite tombstone. A hundred years from now, people will be able to see what you looked like.

It would be wonderful if we could look upon the faces of our ancestors of a hundred years ago. It may not be so wonderful a century from now when our descendants want to know who put them so deep in debt. We could be prime targets for desecration ceremonies.

Ever think what it will take to pay back four trillion or maybe even five trillion dollars if we have to pay it back with dollars at their 1939 value?

We're so used to worrying about billions and trillions, we don't even pick up the millions off the floor anymore.

The government says the unemployment rate increase is down. This fails to point out that the rate is still increasing and jobs are still being lost. In 1933 Americans used to say, "Times is bad." Now times are so good we are only laying off 2,000 to 10,000 more workers every time you turn on the news.

When we have a recession, we do our best to create inflation. When we have inflation, we try to bring on a recession. And it's easy to tell when there is a recession—people have to choose between the boat, the four-wheel drive, and the beach cottage.

But we are a rich nation. You can tell it by watching television. We have million-dollar ballplayers, million-dollar movie stars, million-dollar TV anchors, and million-dollar evangelists. We have lottery winners and quiz show contestants winning limousines and baskets of money, and bundles of fourth-class mail saying we may have won ten million dollars. It makes you feel rich to be around so much green stuff. And you don't even have to pay taxes on it.

Republicans believe in the trickle-down theory. The fellow it's trickling down on doesn't think so much of the idea.

But if you pile a rich man's arms full of cash money, he's bound to drop a bill every now and then, so the man on the street can have a chance to pick one up.

The top 2 percent of America's population controls more wealth than the bottom 90 percent. It's pretty hard to find a Democrat in that top bunch. But there are a lot of Republicans in the bottom ninety percent who think they're in that top 2.

At election time the candidates promise the "middle class" a gravy train, so everyone wants in that category.

The working stiff wants to come up in the world, and the rich suburbanite wants to come along for the ride.

The real middle class is already paying much of the cost of governing, since the folks in Washington cut income taxes on the wealthy and big business and raised the cost of Social Security.

The same middle class is buying medical care for the rest of the country in hospital and property taxes and higher hospital bills to pay for the poor.

Rich sick people call in a top specialist. Poor sick people go to the emergency room or outpatient clinic. It's the ones in the middle who get squeezed.

And that middle class guy can have real problems if he changes jobs and can't get insurance or works for a company that doesn't offer any help. It's even worse if he or his kid has a pre-existing condition. His pre-existing condition is the sinking feeling he gets before they come to take his savings, his car, and his house.

Doctors, medical supplies, hospitals, and treatment are terribly expensive. And new hospitals are being built all the time. Makes you wonder how they can spend so much money on television advertising.

Real estate people, Wall Street brokers, and politicians think low interest rates are the greatest thing since broccoli, but they don't do much for folks living on their savings.

When Wall Street manipulators lose money, it isn't money at all. It's all on paper. It's all on paper when they gang up and buy a company, too. But to the thousands of workers who lose their jobs when their companies are sold off to pay the debt, it's a paper tiger that eats them alive.

Every time Wall Street sneezes, the rest of the country has to go to bed.
But then, a country dominated by Wall Street is condemned to repeat itself.

A long time ago we called the big time banker-industrialists robber barons. Things have changed since then. Those thieves who robbed our great-great-grandfathers were pikers. If today's high-tech thieves had lived back then, we wouldn't have any country left.

We've been in trouble ever since we went off the Gold Standard. We used to keep all our gold locked up at Fort Knox. But it keeps leaking out of the country.

What we ought to do is go on the cocaine standard. It's more valuable than gold. Corner the market and lock it up.

People couldn't use it, and we could issue paper money with cocaine backing it up. Then we'd be as rich as the South American drug lords.

'Hey, man, ain't you heard? We're off the gold standard. Now cocaine's backing up the buck.'

I overheard one worker telling another, "Cheer up.

You may get a raise pretty soon. I hear they're trying to increase the minimum wage."

When it's time to sell his stock, the cowman is at the mercy of the market. His cattle may bring just half the value he'd hoped for, but the price of steaks doesn't go down.

Let a Mideast potentate have a fainting spell and the oil companies raise the price at the pump twelve or fifteen cents a gallon, even when all the storage tanks are full.

Oil company price increases are OK. But if a politician suggests a nickel-a-gallon tax hike, that's a different story.

Then there's the Federal Reserve. The chairman sees dangerous signs that inflation is about to attack, so he comes out and raises his hand.

Interest rates go up, the threat of inflation goes down, the banks get a bigger percentage of your loan money, and Wall Street celebrates.

The Fed turns the economic engine into a teeter-totter.

And it's amazing what makes Wall Street nervous. If employment is up, if the economy is improving, if the outlook is good, then stocks plummet. If jobs are being lopped, if the economy is sagging and the outlook is bad, the stockbrokers and soothsayers are happy as a dog with a hole in the fence.

And now we have something called derivatives.

Billions of dollars fly across the world on electronic beams. Hundreds of millions of dollars are made or lost in a twinkle and nobody can see it.

The economic future of the world could depend on a bunch of young computer jockeys who spend all their time punching keyboards like it was some sort of video game. And very few can "derive" anything good from a crash.

But America is still a land of opportunity—unless you happen to be a young couple trying to buy a house at a price you can afford.

When things look dark to us, though, just think how a refugee from most any other country looks at us after walking through one of our supermarkets. And we wonder why people all over the world would paddle across an ocean to get here!

On Business

Will Rogers said:

"Rival gangs don't murder each other. They are killed by members of their own gang for holding out and for double-crossings. I tell you this system has a lot of merit. Wouldn't it be great if bankers bumped off the crooked ones?"—June 26, 1930

(Big Business) "got big according to law. But not according to Hoyle."—May 30, 1922

"Frank Phillips of oil fame...said...the oil men were going to draw up a code of ethics. Everybody present had to laugh. If he had said the gangsters of America were drawing up a code of ethics, it wouldn't have sounded near as impossible."—July 11, 1933

What Will Might Say Today:

On Business

As I understand it, when the capitalistic system works best, a fella borrows or invests his money, builds a better product or provides a better service, makes his customers happy, and makes a nice profit. And his word is his bond.

Now we seem to have profits without honor.

If they ever get through training Congress in the meaning of ethics, a highly unlikely possibility, they ought to move up to Wall Street. The Indians traded Manhattan Island to the Dutch for a bunch of beads.

Financiers learned a lesson from that. They found they can buy billion-dollar industries with worthless paper. They can pay the rest of it by cannibalizing the company they just bought.

That's like taking a chicken's drumsticks while he's still using them.

First we saw the merge-and-acquire craze by which solid companies were acquired, gutted for hundreds of millions, and left to sink or swim in oceans of debt. Now they keep the company and make it lean and mean by firing people.

The takeover people who do the firing are mean, and the executives and workers they fire are lean.

Industrialists who got rich selling guns, ammunition, and bombs during wartime were scornfully called war profiteers. Now providing the peasants of the world with rockets and explosives has become one of our most respected and lucrative pursuits.

Why, if we quit supplying our armed forces and all those involved in brushfire fights and revolutions all over the world, we'd have to close up shop and put the whole country on welfare.

It's real progress to have nuclear energy producing cheap electricity. Now if we could just afford to pay for those nuclear power plants before they blow up, we could enjoy all the cheap electricity.

Taxes are high. So are electric bills. If they'd make electric bills deductible, we could let the government and the power company fight it out.

We spent a lot of our time watching and worrying about the Communist Party. But it might have been a good idea to find out what our graduate business schools were up to. They've made the capitalistic system a role model for how to be No. 2.

Everybody is worried about the imbalance of trade with foreign countries. Our industrialists made one mistake. Instead of sending American goods overseas, they sent the factories.

And every time we send a factory overseas for "cheap labor," we put our own workers out of work. Pretty soon the people will be poor enough to bring the factories back, and we can start all over again.

The new motto of this country is "Four-to-six weeks." Anything can be fixed in "four-to-six weeks." All parts can be ordered in "six-to-eight weeks." And if the problem can't be solved in that time, it's "on back order."

Read the warranty of any new product carefully. I heard of one that says, "If you have read this warranty, it has expired."

Oil made us the most powerful country in the world. We used up a lot of energy being powerful. Now we're like a drug addict, hooked on oil and at the mercy of the junkie who has plenty of it.

The oil producers squabble and prices come down. We drive big cars. They get together and the price goes up. We drive little cars. It's hard to decide if we'll go to the poorhouse in a Cadillac or a Toyota.

We have a peculiar way of handling our problems. If we have a recession with a lot of people out of work, the first thing we do is lay more people off.

It's easier to cut people than profits.

Even though they're making big profits, a lot of companies downsize, restructure, streamline, fire thousands of workers and hire temporary help. It's a lot cheaper to hire part-timers than pay loyal longtime employees, who'd get decent wages, health care, vacations, and retirement.

It's cheaper to pay a few people overtime and get by with fewer of them. Workers who survive work longer hours and worry about being next on the hit list.

We used to think what mattered was hard work, loyalty, and honesty. Now it's the Bottom Line. If you cross it, you're out.

'The note says, *'Congratulations to each and every employee for our most profitable quarter ever!'*
. . . the other one is a pink slip.'

Cigarette companies have already succeeded in enslaving a good part of the globe with the filthy habit. They used to hand out free samples to draw the flies into their spider trap.

Now it isn't even free. They simply feed the unsuspecting youth a Mickey Finn of added nicotine, and their stockholders' future is enriched.

Maybe we ought to have a federal law against business contributing to the delinquency of minors.

I had my brakes checked the other day, and the mechanic said there was nothing wrong with them. This fellow could be drummed out of the auto-repair business for being disloyal to the profession.

Some of the people most opposed to gambling are farmers, and farmers are the biggest gamblers of all. But losers leaving the table in Las Vegas can't get a federal loan to cover their shortfall.

Bankers have been back of farmers all the way. They've been back of the mortgage, the foreclosure, the auction, and the move back to town.

Comparable worth is one of those modern terms created in the fight for female equality. In other words, a woman should be paid as much as a man when she's doing work equal to his.

Is the work of a garbage collector worth more than that of a secretary? It is if he goes on strike for a month.

The problem with the system is that the harder you work, the less you get paid. The ditch digger works harder than anyone. The foreman who watches him gets twice as much. The boss who doesn't even go to the job gets more than all of them put together.

It's getting plumb ridiculous. Why, some of these CEO's are making almost as much as a basketball player.

The trust busters smashed monopolies years ago. But corporations are gobbling each other up like horned toads on ant hills. They're putting Humpty Dumpty back together again.

If mergers and acquisitions of business keep up at the present rate, we're going to have one great big company and one great big government. And we won't be able to get satisfaction from either one of them.

People who lose money on the stock market say they really didn't lose any money—it was "on paper." Of course, had they cashed in those stocks and bonds before they collapsed, the paper would have been colored like greenbacks.

These are the same people who tell you their car— the same model as the one you're driving— gets thirty-five miles to the gallon when yours is doing good to get twenty.

Insurance companies are friendly people. They hope you stay healthy. They hope you can meet your premium payments and that you drive safely. They worry with you when storms threaten to blow your house down. They're concerned that nobody trips on your front steps or is

consumed by your family dog. They wish you a long life.
And when you die, they send the money you've been saving to your relatives to fight over.

Butchers in the old days used to cut the fat off your steaks and give you free liver and bones for the dog. They wouldn't have anything left if they cut all the fat off now. The liver commands a prime price, and the bone is all ground up to pad out the hamburger.

Filling stations started out as places where you stopped to fill up the gas tank, fill up the radiator, and fill up the tires. Then they became service stations, where attendants checked the tires, cleaned the windshield, swept the carpet, dumped the ash trays, and checked the oil while they dispensed gasoline.
Now you can check your own tires and even pay for the air that used to be so free. The attendants let you have what gas you pay for in advance by pushing buttons in a bulletproof cage. They'll sell you peanuts, magazines, nuts and bolts, and in some states, beer. But they won't move from their secure pillbox.
No. You can't call them service stations any more.

If Wall Street swindlers ever buy your house, you might expect them to give you used shingles, bent nails, and toilet seats as a down payment. Then, to sweeten the deal, they'd cut off the cat's tail and kill the dog.
They'd eliminate electric, water, and sewage service to cut expenses and tear down the fireplace and sell the bricks to ease their payments.
Just when you think you might get a small check, they'd roll over and take bankruptcy and give the whole

thing to a dealer from Japan.

Used car dealers must be the most patriotic people around—they fly the biggest flags.

Ever wonder what happened to good old American enterprise?

What the Japanese didn't appropriate, we've given to the giant discount companies. We go out on the highway and buy cut-rate goods and wonder why the downtown merchant went out of business.

When the local businessman isn't there to buy ads, the presses in the local newspaper stop and the TV station is silent. The businessman, newspaperman, TV people, and the fella from the Chamber of Commerce who invited the discount house to town aren't there to get a haircut or shoeshine or get their suits cleaned, so the barber, the shine man, and the cleaner leave town, too.

They probably carry a suitcase they bought in a discount city.

From the upswing in the auto industry, it looks like the Chief Executive Officers of America have stumbled upon a revolutionary new theory:

Treat the customer courteously and fair, help him find what he needs, listen to his complaints, and do something without referring him to someone else who can't do anything about it.

"Why, yes," they say, "if we're good to the customer, he'll be happy and he'll come back to trade with us again. What a novel idea. Why in the world didn't we think of this before? "

On Congress

Will Rogers said:

"Legislatures is kind of like animals in the zoo. You can't do anything about 'em only stand and watch them anyhow."—April 7, 1935

"Senators are a kind of never ending source of amusement, amazement, and Discouragement. But the Rascals, when you meet 'em face to face and know 'em, they are mighty nice fellows. It must be something in the office that makes 'em so ornery sometimes. When you see what they do officially you want to shoot 'em, but when one looks at you and grins so innocently, why you kinder want to kiss him."

"An awful lot of people are confused as to just what is meant by a 'Lame Duck Congress.' It's like where some fellow worked for you and you let 'em out, but after you fired 'em, you let 'em stay long enough so they could burn your house down." —December 8, 1932

What Will Might Say Today:
On Congress

Britain has its House of Lords, where membership is guaranteed for life. Over here we call it Congress.

Taking real estate from someone who is housed in a concrete pillbox with rockets, machine guns, and land mines at his disposal isn't easy. But it might be easier than taking a seat from a member of Congress who's shaken down every industry and union in the nation to keep hold of it.

There ought to be a cap on how much money a lawmaker can take. When they get so much, they ought to step aside and let someone else in to feed at the trough.

Ethics in this country are strange. Almost every group of robbers has a code of ethics. A code of ethics allows doctors, lawyers, and real estate developers to find the loopholes.

In Congress, the code frowns on taking bribes—but

gifts, tokens of esteem, honorariums, bequests, fees, contributions, junkets, book deals—they're all right.

And we don't issue licenses to steal. That privilege is reserved for lawyers, bankers, and members of Congress.

Things were running pretty smooth for Congresspeople when they could stack cash in the closet, dance on the table, and hide their peccadilloes in the basement.

But with politicians of opposite ilk looking into bedrooms, barrooms, and Swiss banks and calling the TV cameras in, we may have found a way to get some of the lifetime members off that high hill.

We always hear that it's a sign of weakness to compromise. If a leader is willing to meet his opponents in the middle, they say he "caved in" or "waffled."

But this country was built on compromise. That's the way we make our laws. It's a way nations can avoid going to war. Not much gets done when both sides refuse to compromise. Take Congress, for example.

The insurance companies and health-care businesses sure help members of Congress pass their fiscal exams. Every time a health plan is proposed, those businesses contribute to the lawmakers' welfare. And after they've donated, it's the National Rifle Association's turn.

These groups help out the ailing TV networks, too. In $10 million commercials some well-paid actors come on and complain about government meddling.

The housing problem in Washington could easily be solved if they moved all the lobbyists out. But that could be bad—then all the representatives and senators might have to think for themselves.

And lobbies in hotels aren't lobbies anymore. They're "atriums" or "solariums." Congress has given lobbies a bad name.

In 1988 Congress tried to raise its pay $50,000 per member. It got caught, so it came up with a cost-of-living adjustment making them in the top 1.2 percent of wage earners in the nation. Their pay increased five times faster than other workers'.

No wonder they vote with the monied people. They've promoted themselves into the upper crust.

When members of Congress talk about "temporary" taxes, it's not like temporary insanity, when a person is crazy for a minute, then is as nice a fella as you would ever want to meet.

When they say temporary in referring to taxes, they're talking concrete.

When Congress wants to look busy, it starts a big investigation. It seldom investigates itself, where more sinners are doing the devil's work than anywhere on earth.

So you can tell when there's a heat wave in Washington. Many of the members of Congress will be studying the champagne shortage in France.

'Be careful, mon amí. The Congress of the United States is again investigating us.'

Members of Congress open their mouths so much they can't hear the voters back home. They listened more

when travel to Washington was by horse and buggy.
Maybe all the round-the-world jetting has damaged their
hearing.

In the heat of combat, Congress sorta forgets what
bills serve the people. The name of the game is to make
the other side look bad or bring the president down. The
important thing is the Party. The people are the last ones
to benefit from partisan fights.

If something's good for the people, it probably isn't a
good idea. If it's good for Wall Street, well, that's another
matter.

Congress members don't like the idea of doing away
with assault rifles. It'll make it hard for hunters if they
can't squeeze off fifty shots a second.

If a hunter can't hit what he's shooting at with five
shots in a clip, he'd better go back to National Rifle Association boot camp. But I'm not sure you can blame those
folks in Congress for paying attention to voters who carry
both assault weapons and fat wallets.

It's bad enough to have TV bring sex and violence
into our living rooms. But has anybody assessed the
damage that can be done if people take up watching
congressional sessions and committee hearings on C-
SPAN?

It could bring the end of democracy as we know it.

Congressmen have a good retirement, but they have
an even better backup system.

When they retire or lose an election, they go to work

for the people who hired them to start with—the lobbyists.

And now term limitation is popular. But what good will it do?

If the same people vote for the same type of dope they replace, they'll have the same result, only he'll be a beginner with no clout.

Do we really want a whole rookie team as starters?

On Religion

Will Rogers said:

" . . . that's one wonderful thing about the Bible. There was no censorship in those days. Of course now some of our churches hold conferences and cut out certain parts they think don't belong in there, or change them to what they think should be said . . . In other words, we are always having somebody improving on the words of the Lord. That's even worse than a scenario writer brightening up Shakespeare."—June 22, 1930

"Our religious beliefs are many, but one belief is universal with all, and that is that there is some divine being higher than earthly. We can speak to Him in many devious ways, in many languages, but He sees us all in the same light, and judges us according to our actions, as we judge the actions of our children different because we know they are each different."

" . . . every man's religion is good. There is none of it bad. We are all trying to arrive at the same place acording to our own conscience and teachings. It don't matter which road you take."—March 11, 1923

What Will Might Say Today:

On Religion

Jesus was a man of peace and brotherly love, but some self-professed religious groups gather arms and ammo for "Judgment Day." And some priests and preachers say it's okay to kill doctors who perform abortions and anyone else in the area.

Jesus' message gets distorted when heavily armed people kill in His name. Actually they don't use His name very much. They prefer the Old Testament.

They're a lot fonder of vengeance than they are of brotherly love.

If a preacher has more than two Rolls Royces and gold-plated plumbing, he's doing the Lord's work, getting used to the streets of gold in the Hereafter.

No matter how much of a Christian a man is, no matter if he is born again, teaches Sunday school, and reads himself to sleep with the Holy Bible—if he's in the wrong political party, he's automatically a lost, sinful heathen.

Too many preachers who say they've been "born

again" seem to have been born again as politicians.

If all the money sent to TV's political preachers was put to good use, we wouldn't have many people going hungry. And some of those political preachers are likely to have an interesting Hereafter.

Those are the guys who prey on the poor instead of praying for them.

'I've always felt that giving to the poor only corrupts their morals.'

Back during the Industrial Revolution big money-makers were known as robber barons. Factory workers slaved long hours under terrible conditions, for little pay.

Preachers convinced the workers their condition was the will of God, but they'd get their reward in the Great Hereafter, where streets are paved with gold and diamonds and pearls grow on trees.

The Robber Barons are back. And some of the preachers have joined them. They've convinced many poor people they can get a ticket to that Great Hereafter by mailing in their Social Security checks.

Jesus probably wouldn't get a very warm welcome in this day and time—going around preaching for the rich to give up their worldly possessions and for everyone to love the poor and take care of the afflicted.

He might even be branded some kind of wild-eyed nut who probably favors a tax increase.

When we have a problem, everybody gets busy thinking up slogans to solve it. Slogans usually don't make people give up dope or drinking. They don't take automatic weapons away from thugs or make kids go to school.

If you're looking for words that work, you might try the Ten Commandments.

The Guilted Age

Will Said:

> "They say all children reach a 'smart aleck' age some time. Well, our whole country is in that stage now. Every man, every denomination and every organization wants things their way."—December 10, 1930

> "Nobody wants his cause near as bad as he wants to talk about his cause."

> "We will never have true civilization until we have learned to recognize the rights of others."

What Will Might Say Today:

On the Guilted Age

According to a recent book, we lead the Western World in murders, AIDS cases, and divorces. We're behind in voter turnout and two-parent families. We lead in teen pregnancies, drunken driving deaths, and babies who die before their fifth birthday.

We're No. 1 in billionaires, with ninety-six. In solving murders, we're No. 14.

Even if some of the others catch up, our record isn't much to brag about.

We have potato chips, fish and chips, and micro-chips. But the modern thing is the chip on the shoulder.

We've been struck by a national disease—guilt.

For everything we used to feel proud of, there's a reason we should blame ourselves. If the Founding Fathers had had this disease, they'd still be sitting on Plymouth Rock.

If historical characters two hundred years ago could hear how history professors have revised what they did, they'd be plenty surprised—and mad.

And if those rough, tough characters did come back, there'd be some more historical rewriting—real quick.

Poor people work hard to escape the slums they've been locked in. If they get rich, they lock themselves behind walls and guards to keep their former neighbors out, this time without the cockroaches.

It's nice to escape blame for fouling up. Blame your parents. Whatever it is, if they didn't do it, they should have. And if they shouldn't have, then they did.

A modern idea is using city streets as asylums for the mentally ill. It's a lot cheaper than locking those folks up.

And it's not a total loss. Those people and other homeless transients make taxpayers think they're getting their money's worth from libraries, bus and train stations, and other public spots.

Environmentalists are quick to jump on poor countries for cutting down their rain forests and destroying the world's oxygen-producing element.

But we haven't done much for greenery, either, from the amount of it we've buried under interstate highways and parking lots.

And, about those vanishing rain forests—the natives wouldn't have to cut them down if they weren't trying to raise crops to provide powders for Americans to snort up their noses.

If you feel guilty when you squirt a little deodorant under your arms, don't even consider what the airliner you're riding in is doing to the ozone when it belches out tons of hydrocarbons at 35,000 feet.

If you don't believe it could be a problem, stand behind a taxiing airplane sometime. Jets have awfully bad breaths.

We've spent billions for toxic waste cleanup. The poisoned pits didn't get cleaned out, but the taxpayers did.

We seem to have a problem.

Some scientists believe global warming is going to flood the earth. Others think another ice age is on the way. Still others think we'll be cooked when we destroy the ozone layer.

In the meantime, a comet might get us. Earthquakes, cold winters, floods, hurricanes, hot summers—all are indications of something.

Of course, the sun's going to fade out in a few million years. Then we won't have to worry about the other hazards.

Entertainment stars, athletes, talk show hosts, and media personalities are role models, sometimes even called "heroes." They're hailed for victories over alcohol or dope. But celebrity doesn't make a hero out of a rock star, a ball player, or a boxer.

Seems like pollsters and reporters have "heroic" mixed up with "notorious."

A lot of zealots are taking over school boards all over the country and using the public schools to advance their political and religious ideas.

They've stirred up a lot of angry debate, ordering that their beliefs are the ones all children should be taught.

Many of them believe in a literal interpretation of the Bible. Some believe Halloween's goblins and witches are satanism and "Santa" is an anagram of Satan.

If this keeps up, there'll be the devil to pay.

'Get thee behind me, SANTA!'

As we marked the 50th anniversary of the end of World War II, there were more battles over the atomic bombing of Hiroshima and Nagasaki.

Some 1990s scholars portrayed the actions as "war

crimes." They said the Japanese were ready to surrender before the bombs were dropped.

Maybe so, but with Japanese soldiers fighting to the death and Kamikazes sinking so many of our ships, you'd have had a hard time selling that idea to the sailors and Marines around Okinawa in 1945.

And any of those scholars descended from World War II fighting men might not be around today.

After World War I we demanded reparations from the defeated and repayment from our allies. After World War II we, the winners, paid to rebuild the losers, and we've felt guilty ever since.

Strange times we're living in. When some kind of minority becomes the majority, they're still the minority.

And the majority is still the majority even though it's in the minority. You can believe that, because federal courts say it's so.

It's also strange when some ethnic groups shun their successful fellows who grab a share of the American dream. They'd rather pull their fellows down than pull themselves up.

Many reformers start out with the best intentions that go bad.

Take the French. They wanted liberty and equality. They fought for it. They ended up lopping off the heads of the rich, then switched to lopping the head off anyone who disagreed with them.

We have a lot of causists like that. They're all for free

speech until somebody they disagree with is in town. Then they march around hollerin' to keep those folks from having their say.

We've been blessed with freedom to say what we please, but we don't want that privilege applying to just anybody.

Some people who are worried about injustices would have us adopt speech codes on school campuses and laws against jokes that offend one group or another. They think the First Amendment goes too far.

But when we get scared or mad, we have to watch it not to grab at a solution that's as bad as the problem.

Too many people would save the Constitution by tearing it up.

Shooting off your mouth can be more dangerous than shooting off a gun. If you kill someone, you can get off with a good lawyer and a little luck, but if you accidentally offend some group of victims, you'll lose your job, your reputation, and your last friend.

You'll be so deep in disrepute that even your Old Dog Tray won't speak to you.

Of course, the political-correctness police have a point. You shouldn't put someone down because of race, religion, or sex. But they go too far. They'll blow the whistle on everything—even Sesame Street and Disney characters—for hidden insults.

If they can't laugh at cartoons, they should attend the conventions of our two political parties. Neither one of them is correct, but they provide a lot of laughs.

One trouble is that too many causists have no sense of humor. They march in the streets waving their fists in the air, or they fly off the handle and yell at each other. If they'd just learn to laugh at themselves, they'd make a lot more friends, and they might even have some fun doing it.

Of course, some groups demand the hide of anyone who jokes about them. But they stand up and say nasty things about their own people and everyone laughs.

You can't make fun of plumbers or street cleaners or women or short people or tall people or fat people.

You can make jokes about yourself. And if you're short, fat, skinny, bald, or klutzy, you can joke about your condition.

Otherwise you'll have to find your subjects in Congress or the White House.

Minorities are expected to vote for their own, but when white men vote for white men, it's called racist and sexist.

What ever happened to the idea of voting for the best person, no matter what color or sex he or she may be?

You can't argue with anyone who says that slavery is a terrible blot on this country. But I have a friend who has an unusual slant on it. He says he's real happy to be an American.

His grandfather, once a slave, fought for the Union. My friend has been a dentist, an Air Corps officer, and a civic leader.

"If my ancestors had stayed in Africa," he said, "I'd

probably be living under a tree."

Now that's a viewpoint you don't run into everyday.

We all pull together during a major war—it's peace-time we've got to worry about. That's when people really get mad at each other.

This country used to be a "melting pot." Everyone wanted to be a part of the stew. Today the melting pot is an electronic oven that can cook just one hot dog at a time.

If you aren't a victim here, you're not trying.

It doesn't take a lot of talent because victims come in all ages, colors, sizes, sexes, occupations, beliefs, physical conditions, and preferences. Your chances of being a victim are limitless.

If you can get some kindred souls together and create a row, you'll get your chance to snarl in front of a TV camera. That'll gain more recruits and pretty soon you'll be a special interest group and qualify for a fistful of grants.

Who says this isn't the land of opportunity?

Some of our most successful people could have claimed to be a victim of something or another, but they didn't use it for a crutch.

They used it as a stepladder.

The main thing that's wrong with this country is that almost nobody is looking for what's right with it. We don't have many problems that couldn't be cured with good manners and common sense.

Maybe we could start by substituting "need" or "ability" for "race" or "gender" when it comes to handing out financial aid or hiring a new employee.

A friend of mine has the right idea. She was offered a great job because someone told the prospective boss "She's Hispanic, she's a woman, and she's good!"

"I just wish," she lamented, "he hadn't said 'She's good!' last."

It's hard to figure which are worse—the lawyers who have made everyone distrust everybody else or the psychologists who have succeeded in making guilt our greatest natural resource.

Anybody who goes far enough back in history can find an excuse to feel guilty. Everybody has an ancestor or a homeland that has done somebody or some other country wrong.

To cure all the guilt in the world, you'd have to wipe out the human race. But you'd probably miss somebody. And then he'd feel even guiltier about being left behind.

And it's too bad old Christopher Columbus isn't around to defend himself. He wasn't responsible for the behavior of later explorers, and he doesn't deserve the blame for all the ills of the Americas for the last five hundred years.

You can't say Columbus "discovered" America, because people were already here. Some say he just stumbled over America, bringing the plague of European culture with him.

It's true, the Europeans did bad things to natives. Then again, the natives played soccer with their enemies' heads and ripped out the hearts of sacrificial maidens. If you're part Native American, you can feel guilty about that.

Now Berkeley, California, won't celebrate Columbus Day. They celebrate "Indigenous Peoples Day." How does this strike the people in Columbus, Ohio?

Indigenous People, Ohio?

Hail, Indigenous People?

You may recall that Will Rogers said his people didn't come over on the Mayflower, but they met the boat.

I'm not sure Will would answer to "Indigenous."

'Sink those guys, Indigenous Ones, or it's the end of civilization as we know it.'

On Life in General

Will Rogers said:

What's the matter with an age when our biggest gangster is our greatest national interest?"—March 10, 1932

"The funnies occupy four pages of the paper and editorials two columns. That proves that merit will tell."

"This country is not where it is today on account of any one man. It is here on account of the real common sense of the Big Normal Majority."

What Will Might Say Today:
On Life in General

As much as they might like to believe it, the Baby Boomers really didn't invent everything.

And sex education is pretty useless, particularly after the kids have watched cable television.

They've come up with a new type of uplift device to make girls more appealing above the waist. Now if they'd develop a contraption to shut it off below the waist, it might take care of the teen-age pregnancy problem.

Sex used to be something you did but didn't talk about. Today you talk about it and are afraid to do it. Condoms used to be something you whispered to your druggist about. Now they might be a side serving at the Sunday School picnic.

It's a pretty good marriage these days if it lasts until all the wedding gifts are unwrapped.

The modern woman often chooses to keep her own family name instead of taking her new husband's. That should please nosy neighbors who are happy to fear the worst, and it's perfectly acceptable to society.

But anybody who has looked at genealogy can't help but wonder if the great-grandchildren will ask, "Who was that strange woman old grandpa was living with?"

Sexual harassment is bad. It's bad, too, when a fella tries to flirt with a girl and ends up in court. That's not the way courting is supposed to go.

And sexual harassment for leering? That's not entirely new. At one time the U.S. Navy could convict an enlisted man of "silent insubordination" for what he was thinking.

The National Endowment for the Arts has done some peculiar things. In the name of freedom of expression, some artists have taken advantage of a radical interpretation of art to show stuff you don't want your kids to see. Then they holler that their rights are violated when people object to tax money going for their dirty pictures.

The real test of their art should be the free market place. If nobody buys a $150,000 piece of art, chances are pretty good it's not worth $150,000.

It's too bad those exhibitionists give their self-righteous enemies so much ammunition. Those artists may find that their shock waves have brought down museums, symphonies, and public broadcasting.

And that's bad news for Barney and Big Bird.

Some of our comedians go so far they would shock a shipload of sailors. When humor is scraped off the bathroom floor and broadcast to the world, the mainstream becomes a sewer. That's not something you want in your living room.

Young people like their music— loud. But you seldom hear them humming any of their tunes. It's hard to hum and yell at the same time.

We forced loud music on Manuel Noriega to make him surrender in Panama. Then we started subjecting the Cubans to our television. But Castro successfully jammed it. Now if we can learn his secret. . . .

Advertising people think the 39-year-old housewife is doing most of the buying in this country, so they aim their music at the 18-year-old kid.

They need to remember that about three-quarters of the money in the country is controlled by the gray heads.

The pitchmen are missing a new group who grew up in the Depression but were too young to realize it. Their folks worried about money. They never spent a dime they didn't have to, because they knew what hard times were.

But the retiree you see on the road in a $75,000 recreation vehicle towing a $10,000 boat isn't worried about hard times.

He's going to spend his pile before those days arrive or before the kids get in a big fight over it.

Americans are the only people on the face of the earth who will go to the poorhouse in an RV.

People think it's fun to soak the insurance companies. Then they look around and find they've soaked themselves.

It's a good thing Americans don't love their wives as much as they do their automobiles. If they did, nearly every man around would be guilty of bigamy.

There's a trend nowadays to get exercise by walking in shopping malls. The womenfolk have been walking the malls for years. Maybe that's why they outlive men.

Leisure's a wonderful thing—if we just had time for it.

It's getting so cowboys are going to have to take steroids in self defense. The bulls are getting so big and strong on the stuff, the cowboys aren't able to stay on them.

And steaks from those super cows will take your knife away from you if you don't look out. But those roasts and chops aren't for export—the sissies in Europe don't want meat that is stronger than they are.

Europe's rail system is improving all the time. Miss a train over there?

Don't worry.

Another will be by in 15 minutes or so. They keep

autos off the road, and the electric trains don't pollute.

We had good trains, but automakers and oil barons convinced us to build roadways costing millions; and airlines convinced us to take a jet instead.

We fly—then spend hours getting into town from the airport. So the preservation of our train system is a valuable asset to the country and its heritage. Now if they'd just preserve the tracks, we could be on our way.

When people say a virus is going around, you don't know if it's something their kid has or something that has infected their computer.

We use computers to calculate, sort and store information, and send messages. We get on the communications superhighway to find out what we want to know, order whatever we want, and see and hear everything that's going on—all from the same easy chair. No wonder we've forgotten how to write with a pen and figure with a pencil.

The computer is a great boon for both home and business. If something fouls up, it makes a good whipping boy. Of course, the human at the keyboard ran it into the ditch, but everyone accepts the computer as the fall guy.

Scientists can look at the hieroglyphics ancient Egyptians left in the Pyramids and find out what they were up to. Reckon they can open up one of our computers 3,000 years from now and find out about us from the records we're storing?

Computers have a tendency to become obsolete in six months.

Since 1.5 million people are in this country illegally, there's a proposal for a national ID card. We manage to deport only one out of four illegals, but carrying a card around our neck could make the rest of us wonder if our privacy might be violated.

Then again, the credit people already know all about us. We really don't have many secrets. What they don't know, the marketing people do. And on the communications superhighway, we might not be clothed at all.

They say they have a new computer that'll do what you tell it to. It understands voice commands. Most people I know get so frustrated with the thing, they tell it where to go, and I'm not sure the machine wants to go there.

The latest word in publishing comes from Australia. It's an electronic book no larger than a credit card that fits into a screen about the size of a paperback book. One card holds as much information as an encyclopedia. A fellow could carry an entire library in his wallet.

And nobody would have to be quiet in the library anymore, because there wouldn't be any rooms full of books—just a little guard shack with a card file holding all the books in the world.

And with all that paper saved, we could once more have forests growing clear across the continent. But it probably will never sell unless it includes pictures and a laugh track.

We're not real smart in this country. We don't pay attention to anything until it's broke. Pennies for repairs become millions for replacement.

If things aren't going well, just say "Just Say No."

Not many people really want to work at what they do. Otherwise why would they ride golf carts, hire someone to do their yard work, and then pay to join a health club?

If you're about to eat something they tell you is unhealthy, don't worry.
 Next week somebody will be reporting that it's good for you. Worry about any stuff you like that someone says is good for you. Next week, it'll be poison.

Your doctor used to make house calls. Now you're lucky if he makes a phone call.

And about the only people who aren't worried about their health are those who are already planning suicide. There're so many ways to do it—drive, fly, breathe, eat, smoke, drink, swallow, or sniff. That's too many choices. Makes you almost want to shoot yourself.

We mustn't deprive the hunter of his rifle. He's probably invested a considerable sum on a straight-shooting barrel with a fine scope capable of bringing down a buffalo or yak at six hundred yards.
 Most of the time he'd better hit with the first shot, or

the game is gone.

Still, the hunter doesn't need a magazine with a hundred shells in it, unless, of course, the deer's within man-killing range and he needs to fire fifty shots a second. That would make some prime deer hamburger.

And he doesn't need Teflon bullets to kill a deer, unless the creature is wearing a bulletproof vest.

'I told him that vest was a dumb idea.'

The New England hunter who shot a housewife dead as she stood in her own back yard explained that he mistook the white kerchief around her neck for a deer's white tail. He was found not negligent, apparently because the woman should not have been standing in her back yard during hunting season.

No one ever explained why he was shooting at the deer's tail. Deer in other parts of the country have their vital organs at the other end.

Then there was that news item about the woman in San Francisco who filed suit because she claimed a bump she got from a cable car caused her to lose all interest in sex.

There's that lawyer problem again. Women used to just say they had a headache, and streetcars were named Desire.